I Have a Dream

QUINCY JONES

By Stuart A. Kallen

Published by Abdo & Daughters, 4940 Viking Drive, Suite 622, Edina, Minnesota 55435.

Copyright © 1996 by Abdo Consulting Group, Inc., Pentagon Tower, P.O. Box 36036, Minneapolis, Minnesota 55435 USA. International copyrights reserved in all countries. No part of this book may be reproduced in any form without written permission from the publisher.

Printed in the United States.

Cover Photo credit: Wide World Photos
Interior Photo credits: Wide World Photos, pages 19, 22, 25, 28
                      Bettmann Photos, pages 5, 9, 12, 15, 23
                      Archive Photos, page 11

Edited by Jill Wheeler

Library of Congress Cataloging-in-Publication Data

Kallen, Stuart A., 1955-
    Quincy Jones/by Stuart A. Kallen
    p. cm. -- (I have a dream)
    Includes bibliographical references (p. 30)
Summary: Describes the life and career of the man who overcame racist attitudes to become a shining star in America's recording and music production scene.
ISBN 1-56239-571-8
1. Jones, Quincy, 1933- --Juvenile literature. 2. Jazz musicians--United States--Biography--Juvenile literature. [1. Jones, Quincy, 1933- . 2. Musicians. 3. Afro-Americans-Biography. 4. Jazz.] I. Title. II Series.
ML3930.J63K35 1996
781.64'092--dc20
[B]   95-44091
                                        CIP
                                   AC MN

TABLE OF CONTENTS

It's like being in the jungle, but no trees, and no grass. Everything is just iron and concrete. It's like every day is the first day and the last day. - Melle Mel

DOWN ON THE SOUTH SIDE

Chicago is called the "Windy City," and the wind does blow hard there. Sometimes warm—sometimes bitter cold—that wind off Lake Michigan can whistle through the concrete streets. It can blow like a hot trumpet playing on an icy winter's night.

It was to these windy streets that Quincy Delight Jones, Jr. was born on March 14, 1933. His mother, Sarah, had moved to the city to escape the racism of Mississippi. His father, Quincy Delight Jones, Sr., came from South Carolina.

In those days, a great wave of African Americans moved "up North." They left behind the segregation and human rights violations in the South. Newspapers waged campaigns to fill factories in northern industrial cities with black workers. They promised blacks freedom from racial hatred in New York, Philadelphia, Detroit, Cleveland, and Chicago. Throughout the 1920s and 1930s, thousands of families pulled out of their Southern homes and headed North.

African-American author, Richard Wright, wrote about Chicago at that time: "that great iron city, that...mechanical city, amid the steam, the smoke, the snowy winds, the blistering suns...migrants like us were driven...down the paths of defeat; but luck must have been with us, for somehow we survived."

Quincy Jones, Sr. had come to Chicago to find work as a carpenter. He was also a semipro baseball player. Quincy Sr. and Sarah did not expect paradise. But a spell of bad luck kept them from finding even a little happiness.

Sarah Jones began to suffer from chronic mental illness. For most of Quincy Jr.'s life she was either under a doctor's care or in mental institutions. Quincy said as a young boy: "Well I can't depend on mother, because I don't have one. I never knew what it was like to have a mother."

The slums of South Chicago, 1923.

Besides the hurt of his family life, the ghetto on Chicago's South Side was harsh and hopeless. America was suffering through a period known as the Depression. One-third of all white Americans were out of work. Unemployment of black Americans was twice that figure. The poverty and segregation that black families left in the South was just as bad on the rundown South Side. African Americans were denied decent schools and even the most basic jobs. Young people tried to find ways to break loose.

Some kids took out their frustrations in bloody street fights. Quincy talked in later years of seeing knifings and shootings when he was just a small boy. There were also gangs. Quincy wrote in 1959: "I was exposed to all kinds of gangs, 'The Vagabonds,' 'The Giles A.C. Gang,' 'The Dukes and Duchesses.' And believe me, Chicago gangs were *rough.*"

Other kids put their energy into sports—especially boxing. This was the best money given to minority athletes at the time.

People were poor on the South Side, but there was one thing that was constant—music. There was music on the street corners, music in the clubs, and music drifting through the paper-thin walls of the cheap apartments.

Quincy tells of his musical memories: "The music I heard in Chicago was from "house-rent" piano players—long-fingered, elderly cats who just played and ate neck-bones and red beans and rice. I was very aware of this even though I was only 10."

More music entered Quincy's room through a brick wall. Lucy Jackson, who lived next door, took piano lessons every week. Quincy would sit and listen through the wall as her hands glided over the piano keys. This was before stereos, before tape players, and before CD boom boxes. Just the sound of those 88 keys moved Quincy down the path to fame and fortune.

One day in 1943, Quincy and his brothers were having their hair cut. Quincy Sr. arrived at the barber shop with their bags packed. He had bus tickets in his hand. They were heading west to Bremerton, Washington, near Seattle, for a new life.

BLUES AND BEBOP
ALL NIGHT LONG

If people would make an effort to meet more people, inside and outside their own country, then things would be cooler.
—Quincy Jones

*J*ust as they had moved to Chicago in the 1920s, thousands of African Americans moved to the West in the 1940s. When Quincy Sr. decided to go, World War II was raging. Factory jobs producing war materials were available in California and Washington. There was a labor shortage and blacks were welcomed.

On July 4, 1943, Quincy, his father, his brother Lloyd, his stepmother Elvira, and her three children arrived in Bremerton. They all moved into a two-room house on top of a hill. It was in the black section of the city. But it was new and it looked great after the Chicago ghetto.

Quincy was the only black kid in an all-white classroom at his school. He said, "The other kids were wonderful to me. Positively no problems. Completely integrated."

With the fear of the street gone, Quincy decided to go into business. He shined shoes, baby-sat, picked strawberries, delivered newspapers, washed windows, worked at a dry cleaners, and set up pins in a bowling alley.

Quincy also hung around the Sinclair Heights Barbershop. Eddie Lewis, the owner, cut hair, trimmed mustaches, and played the trumpet. When he wasn't hustling new jobs, 12-year-old Quincy would listen. Before long, music replaced all of Quincy's other jobs.

Quincy joined the band in school. He tried playing sousaphone, baritone and alto saxophone, French horn, and the trumpet. He played in every musical group at school—chorus, orchestra, and dance band. In 1947, Quincy made his first public appearance, jamming with a band at the Bremerton YMCA.

When he was 15, Quincy wrote a suite called, "From the Four Winds." He hadn't yet studied music composition, but his imagination was in gear.

As luck would have it, Seattle was a very musical city. It was an international port, and sooner or later, all the big stars passed through. The great black musicians came to play for the African-American men and women who worked in the wartime factories. Quincy hustled his way into shows by helping the musicians carry their instruments. He would sit right down in front and watch—never saying a word. During breaks, Quincy would walk up on stage and study the musician's sheet music. He asked the writers why they did this or how they wrote that. Because he was so smart and so young, the musicians were glad to help him.

The main black music of the time was swing. But a new kind of music—rhythm and blues (R&B)—was taking over. Once again, Quincy was in the right place at the right time. One of the greatest pioneers of R&B was in the Seattle area—Ray Charles.

Ray Charles Robinson was from Albany, Georgia. He had been blind since the age of six. He became an orphan at the age of 15. When he wanted to escape the racism of the South, he pulled out a map and pointed to a random spot. It was Seattle, and soon Ray was on a bus to Washington. Ray and Quincy became friends and started jamming together.

Ray Charles—musician, singer, and composer.

As Quincy says: "Ray was 17 and I was 15. In Seattle he had a trio called the Maximum Trio. He played the blues and bebop all night long. It was a gas! He played all the hip things. And Ray used to write for a vocal group I was with."

Quincy asked Charles how to write jazz. Charles showed him methods for arranging big band music, how to voice horns, and how to write in polytones. Charles also showed Quincy how to read and write in braille—the method of reading with fingers used by blind people. The two musicians remain best friends today.

"I was fascinated," Quincy said, "with how all those instruments, each of them with its own sound, could interweave into the fabric of the song."

Another musical genius working in Seattle was Bumps Blackwell. He was a bandleader whose gigs took him all over the Pacific Northwest. Quincy joined Blackwell's group and got experience playing behind the stars who traveled with the band. One of these stars was musical legend Billie Holiday.

Quincy's life was filled with music. He played from 7 until 10 at night at the white clubs like the Seattle Tennis Club and the fraternity houses at the University of Washington. Then Quincy and the band would jam at the black clubs until two o'clock in the morning. After that, everyone would run down to the Elk's club and play bebop until six or seven in the morning. Quincy was 15 years old.

During this time, Quincy was strongly influenced by legendary jazz greats Count Basie and Clark Terry. Quincy would just slip backstage with his instrument under his arm. He walked quickly, knowing that he'd be mistaken for a band member and he could easily mingle with them. At the time, Basie was the best big-band leader in the world. "He took me under his wing," said Quincy.

"He was my uncle, my mentor, my friend—the dearest man in the world."

Legendary jazz great, Count Basie.

ART FOR ART'S SAKE

*I*n 1950, Quincy won a musical scholarship to the University of Seattle. But if he wanted to grow, he had to leave home. Luckily, Quincy also won a scholarship to Boston's Schillinger House of Music (or Berklee College of Music as it is now known). In the summer of 1951, Quincy and his girlfriend, Jeri Caldwell, moved to Boston. But he knew it was just a stop on the way to the capital city of bebop music—New York City.

In the 1950s there was a world-famous club on New York City's Broadway called Birdland. It was named after the renowned bebop pioneer Charlie "Bird" Parker. The club was a magnet for hipsters,

Charlie "Bird" Parker (right) plays saxophone at New York City's Birdland Club.

geniuses, and promising young players like Quincy Jones. Bebop was a style of music that showed off the skills of the solo player instead of a danceable beat. Musicians experimented, competed, and challenged one another to stretch the rhythm and improvise the melody. Most people didn't "get it" and there wasn't much money in playing it. But bebop was the hippest music in the world at the time. Players said it was "art for art's sake."

Bebop moved so fast that unsteady players were swept off the bandstand. Quincy struggled to match the music's tough standards with his solo skills.

Bebop wasn't just a sound, it was an attitude. Beboppers wore the sharpest clothes (called vives) and ultra-hip dudes like Dizzy Gillespie sported berets and goatees. Many of the musicians used drugs.

The world was not friendly to the bebop scene. People couldn't dance to the music. Quincy says: "Miles Davis, Dizzy, Charlie Parker, Thelonious Monk, Charlie Mingus, all the bebop dudes...thought it was unhip to be successful. But the public rejected them—they didn't make a dime, not a dime. And we ended up with a lot of casualties—a lot of people in the gutter dying from heroin."

Quincy did not like drugs. And he needed money. So the 19-year-old quit school and joined up with big-band superstar Lionel Hampton. Big band was the total opposite of bebop. Hampton played the vibraphone and wore outlandish purple outfits. He made crowds of people cheer and dance. Quincy said Hampton's was the first rock & roll band, with a honking tenor sax and screaming trumpet. Hampton toured the South, playing tent shows that featured tap dancers, vocal quartets, and comics.

Quincy played off and on with Hampton from 1951 to 1959 touring every city and every state in America. In 1953, Quincy went with Hampton to Europe where sophisticated crowds loved their jazz efforts. Back in New York, Quincy produced and arranged for dozens of other black musicians. Meanwhile, R&B was growing into rock & roll.

By the mid-1950s, Quincy was practically living in recording studios writing charts for singers and bands. He worked with gospel pioneer James Cleveland, Benny Carter, Dinah Washington, Johnny Mathis, and others. His reputation was snowballing. He discovered sax player Cannonball Adderley. Soon he was writing scores for television shows.

MR. VICE PRESIDENT

*Q*uincy Jones was a shining star in America's recording and music production scene, which was set in New York at the time. But the daily grind of studio work was made worse by the racism he faced every day. Black arrangers were allowed to supervise rhythm and horn sections. But they were not allowed to produce string instruments. Strings were thought of as sophisticated, and many studio executives would not even let them play on black musical numbers. Not only was this an insult to Quincy, but it cut into his income. Often, second arrangers were brought in to do the strings.

In 1957 a break came from Europe. Barclay Disque in Paris asked Quincy to head its musical operations. There was little prejudice in France against blacks. Before long, Quincy won awards in Sweden, Germany, and France for conducting and arranging.

By 1961, rock & roll had taken over America's airwaves. It was mostly white music produced by white producers. There were no black executives. But Mercury Records asked Quincy to join as a talent developer. In 1962, Mercury promoted him to be the first black vice president in the business. That same year, Quincy won his first Grammy Award for scoring Ray Charles's "I Can't Stop Loving You" for Count Basie.

Quincy Jones, recording star, arranger, and composer, 1970.

Quincy worked hard for Mercury. He flew 250,000 miles in 1963 working for Mercury in Holland, Italy, Great Britain, and Japan. During that period, rock & roll was growing into a huge industry. The way music was played and recorded was changing almost daily. People playing electric guitars, electric basses, and drums were cranking out hits on modernized recording equipment. This changed the job for people working in the studio.

In the 1950s, the arranger controlled the recording session. With the new techniques, the producer took over controlling the technical aspects of the record. New techniques included multi-tracking and overdubbing. This involved recording one performance, then playing it over a previously recorded track. This allowed a producer to build dense layers of sound using electronics instead of musicians.

At the same time, black musicians finally were being recognized for their talents. Soul music from Memphis, Detroit, New Orleans, and Chicago was breaking into white radio markets.

Quincy was known for his musical abilities. But no one thought he could produce top-ten hits that sold in the millions. Then one day at a meeting, Quincy heard a demo tape from a Long Island teenager named Leslie Gore. "She was the first young artist I'd heard sing in tune in a long time," he later recalled. Within a year, Quincy had produced a run of top-ten singles with Gore including "It's My Party (and I'll Cry if I Want To)," "Judy's Turn to Cry," and others.

Many of his old bebop friends felt Quincy had "sold out." But he didn't seem to care. The same year that Gore was topping the charts, Quincy produced stellar big-band swing records for Basie and superstar Frank Sinatra.

As a child, Quincy always had been fascinated with movies. As his production credits piled up, Quincy thought about writing for Hollywood films. This was years before the movie industry worked hand-in-hand with top-ten musicians. All of Quincy's Gold Records and Grammy Awards got him nowhere in Hollywood. But he broke into the business when he scored the soundtrack for an independent film called *The Pawnbrokers.*

In 1965, Quincy left Mercury and moved to Hollywood. He was determined to make it in the movie business. It was a brave move. No other African American had broken that racial barrier. The first year was tough. He finally was hired by Universal Pictures to score a movie with Gregory Peck called *Mirage.* But the studio did not know Quincy was black. He almost lost the job when they found out. After a short battle, they let him stay. His talent and dedication soon found him more work.

Quincy was the first arranger to use a synthesizer—on the theme for NBC's detective show "Ironside." Between 1966 and 1969, Quincy spent most of his time in dark screening rooms watching rough cuts of movies and TV programs. He usually was the only black person around. But other African Americans were breaking into the business. Bill Cosby, a comic from Philadelphia, starred on NBC's "I Spy," making him the first black dramatic actor on TV. At the same time, West Indies-born Sidney Poitier was proving that white audiences would pay to see a black actor. In 1967 Poitier was one of America's top box-office attractions.

Quincy, Poitier, and Cosby were having a mini civil rights revolution in Hollywood. By 1970, Quincy had scored four Poitier movies—*In the Heat of the Night, For the Love of Ivy, The Lost Man,* and *Brother John.* Quincy also wrote the theme for Cosby's first sitcom on NBC.

The work was everything Quincy loved. He used large orchestras to highlight the action in the film. He added R&B phrasing to build dramatic tension in the movie. He used music as humor in comic movies such as Goldie Hawn's *Cactus Flower.*

Quincy's fame brought him close to civil rights legend Dr. Martin Luther King, Jr. He jet-setted around the world partying with the rich and famous. Remembering his roots, he recorded an album with some old friends called *Walking in Space.* He later won another Grammy for that album—the best jazz performance by a group.

BODY HEAT AND BRAIN DRAIN

*B*y the summer of 1974, Quincy was at the peak of his career. He had just released the bestselling album *Body Heat.* And he had a new girlfriend—actress Peggy Lipton from the TV show "Mod Squad." But he had constant, throbbing headaches. Quincy had a bubble in the vein that supplies blood to the brain. It's called an aneurysm (AN-yir-izz-em). The bubble finally burst, spilling blood at the base of the brain. Quincy said he felt like someone shot his head off and his life was leaking out of his body. He scheduled two operations between his recording sessions.

In August, surgeons went in and fixed the aneurysm. In September he married Peggy Lipton. He also was awarded a Gold Record by A&M Records for selling 500,000 copies of *Body Heat.* In October, brain surgeons operated a second time. They used pins to hold his skull in place and told him to quit playing trumpet. The pressure would be too great and might injure him again. The odds of him surviving the second operation were only 1 in 100. After it was over, doctors also told him to rest and take it easy. He did, but not for long.

Quincy Jones writing music in his home studio, 1974.

Before long, Quincy was back at it. The strides in civil rights made during the 1960s were starting to pay off in the mid-1970s. A golden era of black music was in full swing. Black listeners began to buy albums on a mass scale. Political lyrics replaced songs about love and dancing. African rhythm instruments appeared at recording sessions. Synthesizers and electronic effects radically changed the sound of music. Artists like Stevie Wonder and Marvin Gaye signed record-setting, multi-million-dollar recording contracts. Jazz and bebop merged with rock and R&B to create fusion music. Quincy produced the Brothers Johnson and received his first Platinum Record with sales over one million.

In 1977, ABC-TV ran a six-part series called "Roots." It followed author Alex Haley's family through 400 years. "Roots" showed the horrors of slavery and discrimination from Africa to modern America. Haley and Quincy had been friends since the Mercury days, so it was natural that he was called on to score the show. Quincy used African chants and rhythms in the production. When shown, the series had the highest viewer ratings in history. It was the first time many Americans had heard the roots of modern music in ancient African rhythms.

As Quincy said: "African music had always been regarded as primitive and savage. But when you take time to study it you see that it's as structured and sophisticated as...classical music; instruments that are plucked, instruments that are beaten, and instruments that are blown with reeds. And it's music from the soil—powerful. From gospel, blues, jazz, soul, R&B, rock & roll, all the way to rap, you can trace the roots straight back to Africa."

OFF THE WALL AND THRILLER

At that time Quincy also worked on a film called *The Wiz.* It was an African-American version of *The Wizard of Oz.* Quincy was not that thrilled with the project and didn't like the music. But while working on *Wiz* he was introduced to Michael Jackson. Within a few years, Quincy and Jackson would change musical history.

Before the work of the film started, Jackson went to Quincy's house for a rehearsal. Quincy thought he was cute and shy.

Jackson asked Quincy, "Can you find me a producer?" Quincy said, "Yeah, Michael, later, I'm busy right now." But Quincy was impressed with Jackson's knowledge of music. Finally Quincy said, "You got a producer—I'll produce it."

In 1979, Michael Jackson was not a mega-star. He was 19 years old and his last solo hit was "Ben" recorded five years earlier, when Jackson was 14. In 1978, the Jackson's had sold one million copies of the song "Shake Your Body," which put Michael's voice back on black radio. But their sales were nothing compared to their debut as the Jackson Five in 1969. Many wondered if Michael would ever make it as a solo star. But they wouldn't wonder too much longer.

Quincy assembled a studio band from the Brothers Johnson and Rufus, another band he produced. He put together a state-of-the-art pop album blending disco rhythms, pop tunes, and clever arrangements. Michael's fantastic singing soared above it all.

Michael Jackson and Quincy Jones share the spotlight after being honored at the 26th annual Grammy Awards, 1984.

Stevie Wonder and Quincy Jones record
"Stop, Don't Pass Go," 1987.

The album, *Off the Wall,* eventually sold more than seven million copies. And this was before albums were promoted with videos on MTV.

In 1984, pop music climbed even higher. It was a new age of computerized digital recording, cable TV, MTV, and music videos. Quincy had come a long way since the days of fighting to write for string sections. He formed his own record label, Qwest. He won Grammys every year. He helped raise money for Jesse Jackson's historic run for president. And he made another album with Michael Jackson—*Thriller.*

While Jackson composed the breakthrough singles, "Billy Jean" and "Beat It," Quincy put together a team of seasoned recording professionals. When it was done, *Thriller* broke all sales records, selling more than 40 million copies.

WE ARE THE WORLD

*O*nly a producer of Quincy Jones's talents and connection could have put together the all-star cast for "We Are the World." The project was coordinated under the USA for Africa organization to raise money to feed starving people in Ethiopia.

In 1985, 40 of the biggest recording stars in the world gathered in a recording studio in Los Angeles. Before them they had the song "We Are the World," written by Michael Jackson and Lionel Richie. Bruce Springsteen, Paul Simon, Willie Nelson, Diana Ross, Stevie Wonder, Cyndi Lauper, and Bob Dylan were there. But they were only available for one session. The song had to be done right the first time—no retakes.

Quincy was nervous. He had to blend the styles of 40 artists who came from varied backgrounds of rock, country, folk, soul, and R&B. Quincy stood in the middle of the room packed with every great star of the day and blended their voices like he had blended instruments for 30 years. The record sold millions.

But while the world was celebrating Quincy Jones as the undisputed king of pop production, his life was spinning out of control. His marriage to Peggy Lipton had collapsed. He moved to a tropical island and fought off a nervous breakdown.

The natural beauty of the South Pacific island helped restore his soul. Soon Quincy was back in Los Angeles producing Jackson's next album, *Bad.*

BACK ON THE BLOCK

*F*or years, Quincy had talked of recording a multi-disc set that would be a history of African-American music. He wanted the album to go from rock's roots in West Africa right up to rap. He began work on the project in 1988, and its central focus was hip hop. Hip hop and rap are built around the rhymes of performers and the scratchy noise from manipulating vinyl records on turntables. Many people hated the music.

But Quincy saw rap artists like Run DMC, L.L. Cool J, and the Beastie Boys as outlaws. To Quincy they were like the bebop artists he had played with in the 1950s. They defied authority, spoke out against prejudice, and had their own language and dress.

Quincy Jones holds an armful of Grammy Awards.

The album was called *Back on the Block.* It combined traditions of African storytellers, smooth Brazilian music, and rowdy rap. Track by track the album carried the listener through musical history. Ray Charles sang with Chaka Khan. Ice-T rapped with Melle Mel and Kool Moe Dee.

Quincy was never one to let modern technology pass him by. The composer/producer/artist has a fistful of Grammys, TV Emmys, and a few Oscar nominations. He has long been a force in multimedia entertainment, producing works for records, video, movies, and television. In 1995, with a release from his QD7 company, Quincy explored the entire history of music. "We're talking about 479 A.D. through today," said Jones, laughing. Jones also said that he had been working on the project for 20 years. CD-ROM was a perfect medium for the project.

The disc was set in a "virtual juke joint." Users wandered through 3-D rooms like those Quincy found in the music clubs while growing up. Users listened to music in the stage area. They sat at the bar and listened to Dizzy Gillespie talk or played at the pool tables in the game room.

The rooms came alive as a spirit named "Q" led visitors through time. Every wall, nook and cranny told a different story. There were historical movie footage and photographs as well. Interviews were conducted with a large slate of artists from swing, blues, jazz, rap, and more. Q provided visitors with important songlists so they could learn more later. The CD-ROM linked with other CDs so that the visitor could get explanations to music as it played.

THE ONE AND ONLY

*T*here has never been another Quincy Jones. He was born during the Depression, when many poor people did not even own a radio. He saw the coming of TV and the explosive growth of the music industry. Quincy was there at the beginning when swing and jazz were in their early years. He wrote and produced movie scores, pop mega-hits, and interactive CD-ROMs.

But it wasn't easy. His personal life took a heavy toll for his stardom and riches.

Quincy has shown us all that you need a dream. And you need more. In the early years he worked endless hours for little money. He faced down prejudice and racial hatred. He fought death when his brain began to bleed. Yet he finished every project he started. And he succeeded.

Quincy Jones has shown us all that with hard work, honesty, and dedication, we may all have our dreams come true.

The incredible Quincy Jones.

GLOSSARY

Arranger - the person who takes a piece of music and writes out separate parts for each section of the band, such as the horns, strings, rhythm section, and vocal harmonies.

Bebop - a style of free-form jazz music where each player plays intricate solos, blending rhythms and melodies.

Braille - a system of lettering used by blind people in which raised dots on paper are read using the fingers.

Civil Rights - the rights of people to full equal treatment in legal, social, and economic areas.

Depression - a period in U.S. history when the economy performed very badly and there was large-scale unemployment.

Ghetto - a section of a city where a certain class of people are forced to live, either by law or by economic conditions.

Gold Record - a record that has sold more than 500,000 copies.

Hipster - a person who is in touch with the latest styles.

Jamming - playing music.

Platinum Record - a record that has sold more than one million copies.

Polytones - music played in two different keys that compliment each other.

Prejudice - an unfavorable opinion about a person or a group formed without knowledge of that person or group.

Producer - a person who organizes all aspects of a record, play, movie, or television show.

R&B - rhythm and blues music, an urban form of blues usually played with a band.

Racism - a dislike or hatred of people because of their race or ethnic background.

Segregation - separations. Laws that keep black people from free association with white people.

Swing - a smooth, flowing style of big band jazz music that was very popular in the 1930s.

Vibraphone - a musical percussion instrument resembling a large xylophone.

BIBLIOGRAPHY

Gillen, Marilyn A. *Billboard Magazine.* May 20, 1995.

Horricks, Raymond. *Quincy Jones.* Kent, England: Spellmount Ltd., 1985.

Ross, Courtney Sale, editor. *Listen Up: The Lives of Quincy Jones.* New York: Warner Books, 1990.

Time-Life Books. *Creative Fire.* Alexandria, Virginia, 1994.

INDEX

31

DATE DUE

$15